Contents

Exploring Our Environment 4
We All Want Oil 7
Ships, Clean and Leaky 9
On the Rocks 10
Blowouts and Bombs 12
Oil Pollution at Sea 15
Oil Pollution on Land....................17
Cleaning Up the Mess 18
A Gallon of Prevention 21
Hard Lessons 22

More Books to Read 23
Places to Write 23
Glossary 23
Index 24

Words printed in **boldface** type the first time they occur in the text appear in the glossary.

Exploring Our Environment

Look around you. You see forests, oceans, deserts, and beaches. You see farms, factories, and cities. All of these things make up our **environment**. Sometimes there are problems with the environment. For example, have you ever noticed clumps of a black, sticky substance on the shoreline of a lake or ocean? This beach tar is a sign that the water has become polluted with oil. Most oil **pollution** comes from things people do. Why is there oil on our beaches? Let's find out.

4

We All Want Oil

Oil is one of our most valuable natural resources. Most people fuel their cars with gasoline, which is made from oil. Some people use oil for heating. Oil is the main ingredient in plastics, waxes, and many other products.

Oil is pumped out of the ground from oil wells. Oil wells are also drilled in the ocean floor. But not every country has its own supply of oil. Many countries must **import** oil to make the fuels and other products people want.

Ships, Clean and Leaky

Oil is transported around the world in huge ships called tankers. Oil tankers discharge oil, sometimes by accident, sometimes on purpose. For example, to clean out an empty tanker, the crew pumps seawater through the oil tanks. They flush this oily water into the sea, polluting the ocean. Accidental oil spills also cause pollution. If a tanker runs into a coral reef, a rocky shore, or the harbor bottom, the collision can rip a huge hole in the hull. Oil pours out of the ship, forming a thick, black scum that floats on the water.

On the Rocks

Some shipwrecks cause massive oil spills. In 1989, a **supertanker**, the *Exxon Valdez*, ran aground along Alaska's coast. By the time the ship stopped leaking into the pure waters of Prince William Sound, 11 million gallons (42 million liters) of oil had fouled the sea.

Ten years earlier, another supertanker, the *Amoco Cadiz*, got stuck on the rocks off the French coast. This shipwreck released almost 65 million gallons (247 million liters) of oil into the stormy sea.

Blowouts and Bombs

In addition to shipwrecks, drilling for oil in the ocean causes problems. With some oil wells, tremendous pressure builds up underground. The oil may suddenly burst through the pipes, causing a **blowout**. It can take months to bring the gush of oil under control.

Not all oil spills are accidental. During the Persian Gulf War in 1991, two tankers were deliberately bombed. Each side blamed the other for the oil spill, which fouled the gulf coast and threatened local water supplies.

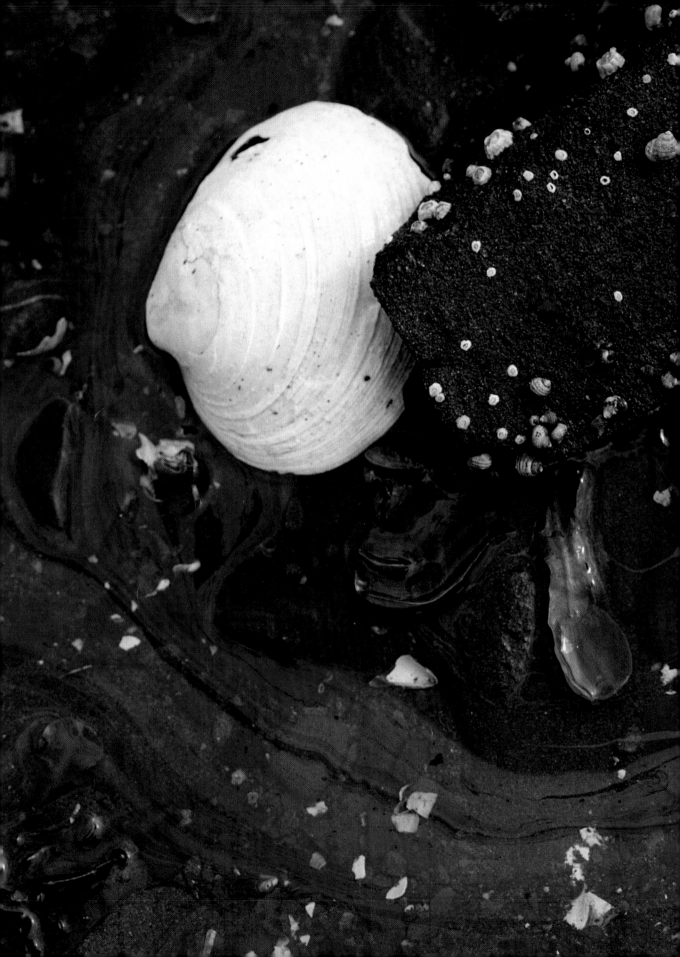

Oil Pollution at Sea

An oil spill results in a smelly, greasy film floating on the surface of the water. Such an oil slick may be small and break up easily, or it may spread for miles and remain intact for weeks. Oil slicks kill many tiny **organisms** floating on the surface of the ocean. Fish that take in oily water through their gills die from lack of oxygen. Oil-coated **sediments** that sink can harm the living things on the ocean floor. Clams, oysters, and starfish all may be poisoned.

Oil Pollution on Land

When an oil slick washes in to shore, the beach becomes covered with a slimy scum. Shorebirds get coated with oil, which soaks into their feathers. This weighs the birds down and makes it difficult for them to fly. They may drown or starve to death.

Sea otters also suffer if their fur gets soaked with oil. With its fur plastered to its skin, the otter's coat no longer keeps it warm. The otter may die from the cold.

Cleaning Up the Mess

People put a tremendous effort into cleaning up large oil spills. They spray chemicals on the slick to break it up. They use special boats to skim oil from the water. They might even burn the oil to get rid of it.

But oil still washes to shore. Volunteers must work day and night to clean up an oil-soaked beach. They have to dig up and dispose of the oily sand. They must scrub oil stuck on rocks. They must also rescue oiled animals and birds and treat them in animal hospitals.

A Gallon of Prevention

Oil spills are a tragedy for everyone. **Toxic** fumes place the ship's crew in great danger. People living near the oil-soaked shore see their favorite places ruined with pollution. The environment may take years to recover.

The best way to deal with oil spills is to prevent them in the first place. Companies need to buy the safest, strongest tankers for shipping oil. Sailors working on the ships and people monitoring the coasts have to keep a close watch on tankers to help them sail safely.

Hard Lessons

No matter how much money is spent on clean-up and no matter how many people volunteer to help, nothing can control the damage from a huge oil slick. By using the Sun and other sources of **renewable** energy, we can reduce our need for oil. And with careful planning and controls, the risk of such spills can be reduced.

More Books to Read

Oil! Getting It, Shipping It, Selling It by Elaine Scott (Warne)
Spill! The Story of the Exxon Valdez by Terry Carr (Franklin Watts)
Save the Earth! An Ecology Handbook for Kids by Betty Miles (Knopf)
Dying Oceans by Paula Hogan (Gareth Stevens)

Places to Write

Here are some places you can write to for more information about oil and oil spills.   Be sure to tell them exactly what you want to know about.   Give them your full name and address so that they can write back to you.

Greenpeace USA
1436 U Street NW
Washington, D.C.   20009

Alaska Center for the
   Environment
519 West 8th Avenue
Anchorage, Alaska 99501

Greenpeace Foundation
185 Spadina Avenue, 6th Floor
Toronto, Ontario   M5T 2C6

Glossary

blowout: the sudden burst or escape of a trapped material.

environment (en-VIE-ron-ment): the surroundings in which a plant, animal, or human lives.

import (IM-port or im-PORT): to bring from another country for trade or sale.

intact (in-TAKT): having all parts; whole.

organism (OR-gah-nih-zuhm): a living plant, animal or individual.

oxygen (AHKS-ih-jhun): a gas that is needed by plants and animals to live. It is colorless, odorless, and tasteless.

pollution (poe-LOO-shun): the spoiling of air, soil, or water with wastes or garbage.

renewable (ree-NEW-ah-bull): able to be made new again.

sediments (SE-duh-mentz): material that settles to the bottom of a liquid.

supertanker: a ship that is equipped with tanks for carrying large amounts of liquid.

toxic (TOCKS-ik): poisonous.

Index

Alaska 11
Amoco Cadiz 11
animals, effects of
    oil spills on, 15,
    17, 18

blowouts 12

environment 4, 21
Exxon Valdez 11

France 11

oil
    clean up of 18
    slicks and spills
        15, 17, 18, 22
    uses of 7
    wells 7
oxygen 15

Persian Gulf War 12
pollution 4, 9, 15,
    17, 21

renewable energy,
    sources of 22

sediments 15
shipwrecks 9, 11, 12
Sun 22

tankers 9, 11, 12
toxic fumes 21